TOGETHER
WE CAN TURN TIDES

A Manifesto to Save the
Oceans, Planet & Ourselves

JEROEN VAN DE WAAL

DID YOU KNOW? 97% of the earth's water can be found in our oceans[2].

I live in fear of what will happen to our planet and our children. Global warming, pollution, poverty, destruction of crucial habitats – they all look like massive threats and problems that are beyond salvation. I cannot accept this and I do not believe this is true. In the worst case scenario, famous scientists all seem to agree that the planet will take care of itself, survive, re-form and recover. It is the human race and many other species that will be beyond salvation.

As a young child growing up in the Netherlands, close to the German border, I was kept awake at night by my fears of SS20 nuclear cruise missiles. These were placed just 20 kilometres away from our house to counter the former East Bloc nations. The never-ending Palestine/Israeli conflict in the Middle East made me afraid for the future. Scary news stories were brought to me by television and newspapers.

Today, global threats, conflicts and misery seem to have increased 1,000 times since my childhood days. Part of this problem is the relentless distribution of news, good and bad, via thousands of media channels. This has an enormous impact on children, and adults too. The sheer amount of information is beyond the imagination and processing capabilities of most people. It beats the hope out of young souls and depresses society.

This absurd increase in mass media channels and our exposure to them, combined with a series of destructive global events, puts many people into a stagnant and complacent 'destiny is doomed' mode. I believe this is the worst possible scenario.

 DID YOU KNOW? Around 30% of all CO_2 emissions produced by humans are absorbed by the oceans[3].

Jacques Cousteau

There is an urgent need to understand the effects humans are having on the marine ecosystems. One model for understanding the ecosystems of the oceans is to think about four inter-dependent types of species, which are all crucial to the efficient running of the ocean. When they are out of balance, one piece is missing, destroyed or is over-abundant, the whole system is damaged and will eventually stop working.

The four species types that are crucial to an ecosystem's survival are: 'umbrella species', which are migratory and cover a large habitat; 'keystone species', which are unique and play a crucial role in maintaining the ecosystem; 'foundation species' that create the habitat, like coral; and 'indicator species', which are sensitive to the environment. Some species will fall into more than one category, such as coral, which plays a significant role as a keystone, foundation *and* indicator species.

Let's look at keystone species. Keystone species are plants or animals, such as coral or beavers, that significantly alter the habitat around them and in turn affect large numbers of other organisms. They play a unique and crucial role in the way an ecosystem functions. While all species in an ecosystem rely on each other, without keystone species the ecosystem would be dramatically different or cease to exist altogether.

Robert T. Paine, an American zoology professor, demonstrated in 1969 how removing one species, the *pisaster ochraceus* sea star, from a tidal plain on Tatoosh Island in America had a huge effect on the surrounding ecosystem. The sea stars eat the mussels on Tatoosh Island. Without the sea stars, the mussels took over and crowded out other species.

The sea star was the keystone species and its disappearance started a domino effect where other species could also disappear and become extinct. The ecosystem in nature cannot support an unlimited number of animals due to competition for food and water resources.

Keystone Species

The Foundation Species

Umbrella Species

Indicator Species

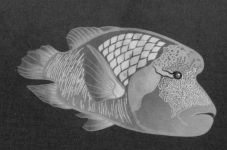

You can see how complex and inter-connected the different species and habitats are. Our every interaction with the oceans, whether directly or indirectly, has consequences. The marine ecosystem is being disrupted. Invasive species have been introduced, such as lionfish in the Caribbean, Asian carp and 'snakeheads' in the USA, coupled with population booms of certain species, such as the crown-of-thorns starfish and types of sea jellies due to the sudden drop in numbers of their predators. This ecosystem disruption leads to the collapse of various fish stocks.

Let's take a quick look at the main causes of marine habitat loss and destruction.

When there is extra carbon dioxide in the air, the water absorbs much of it. The water gets contaminated and its heat rises beyond the expectations of life. When the ocean temperatures rise, there are many adverse effects in the aquatic environment.

Climate change-related heat is melting the icecaps. Ocean ice (or the ice shelf) is already in the sea so it won't affect the sea levels when it melts. Ice sheets lying on the Antarctic continent could cause a sea level rise of up to 60m, but that may take many centuries to occur[5]. However, those melting ice shelves may allow the glaciers to slide off land and into the sea. Melted ice caps and glaciers contaminate the oceans and threaten the life of aquatic plants and animals.

The increase in temperature also limits the concentration or the solubility of oxygen in the water. Plants and animals will then suffocate. These changes of water contamination and temperature lead to marine habitat loss and destruction.

EFFECTS OF MARINE HABITAT LOSS AND DESTRUCTION

When the marine habitat is destroyed or near to vanishing, it has various effects, including a reduction in the water's oxygen concentration to the extent that it can barely support aquatic life. Many plants and animals die. Others may be forced to migrate when they sense changes in their environment.

Humans depend on sea creatures such as octopuses, salmon and tuna for food. When these are depleted, we suffer from the negative impact. Animals like killer whales and sharks depend on other aquatic life, such as seals, for food. Extinction of one means the extinction of the others in the food chain. Marine habitat loss and destruction leads to death and migration of animals.

Some plants and creatures die and become extinct due to extreme eco-logical conditions. The disappearance of, or a decrease in, water masses due to construction or human migration and settlement causes more than just the loss of coastal natural beauty. Encroaching on or destroying natural habitats also means some species of animals and plants may dis-appear entirely.

Coastal regions are major tourist attractions. The sandy beaches, pic-turesque views, aquatic plants and animals, and ocean activities such as scuba diving all play crucial roles for communities to earn a living and governments to collect taxes. When aquatic animals and plants are ren-dered extinct, the beauty of these places is reduced, decreasing tourist activities and causing a loss in livelihoods and revenue.

Some countries have programmes of shark culling using shark nets and drumlines (baited hooks). In Australia, in a twelve-month period to August 2014, 667 sharks, including endangered species such as the great white and grey nurse, were killed. About 100 dolphins, turtles and dugongs were unintentionally killed too. Western Australia also hired shark hunters to kill large sharks, specifically great white, tiger and bull sharks over three metres long, in authorised 'kill zones'.

 DID YOU KNOW? 80% of Australians are opposed to the shark culling, don't fear shark attacks and do feel safe in the sea[7].

Many sharks are slaughtered for their fins. Some people believe that shark fins make great soup and are a medicinal cure for ailments, but the shark flesh has a low value and is discarded. To reduce the load the fishermen have to transport, they take the fins at sea and throw the heavy bodies back into the water. Sharks are caught, dragged on board a boat, their fins are sliced off, then they are thrown back into the ocean – alive. The shark is unable to swim and slowly sinks towards the bottom where it is eaten alive by other fish, suffocates or bleeds to death.

 DID YOU KNOW? There are 73 million sharks killed every year by people to make soup[8].

The shark finners don't care what shark they catch. They fin and kill any species, size or age – even babies. The shark finners use longlines to catch the sharks, and are the most significant cause of losses in shark populations worldwide.

 DID YOU KNOW? Sharks cannot swim backwards.

Shark fins are one of the most expensive seafood items in the world. One kilo of shark fin can sell for more than US$400. Once the fins have been sliced off the shark, they are sent to market, with more than half of the shark fin trade going through Hong Kong. In 2008, the top exporters of shark fins to Hong Kong were Spain, Singapore, Taiwan and Indonesia.

WHY IS THIS A PROBLEM?

The effects of shark fishing can be seen with the loss and devastation of shark populations around the world. Within a decade, most species of sharks will be lost because of longlining[9]. The culling of sharks has an impact on both targeted and non-targeted threatened shark species, with a serious impact on non-target species killed as 'by-catch' (unwanted marine creatures trapped by commercial fishing) such as dugongs, dolphins and turtles.

Sharks are predators and scavengers, helping to eliminate diseased and genetically defective animals and stabilise fish populations. It is difficult to predict what will happen if sharks become extinct. However, when shark populations decrease, a ripple effect will spread throughout the rest of the ecosystem.

As an example, the removal of sharks will increase octopus populations, which means more octopuses will eat lobsters. In Tasmania, the spiny lobster fishery collapsed because the loss of the smooth hammerhead caused its prey, rays, to increase. The larger ray population now eats more scallops, clams and other bivalves, which reduces the bivalve populations, impacting the biodiversity of the ecosystem and harming fisheries.

 DID YOU KNOW? Sharks are a keystone species and their decline will have a major impact on the health of the ocean ecosystem.

This is a type of unsustainable fishing, which we'll look at in more depth later. The massive number of sharks harvested and lack of discrimination about age, sex and size of the shark is depleting populations faster than their reproductive abilities can replenish them. To exacerbate the problem, local sustainable fishermen are driven out of their waters by larger invading industrial foreign fishing vessels.

DID YOU KNOW? Many sharks take up to fifteen years to reach maturity and produce just one pup per year.

This threatens the stability of marine ecosystems. It also threatens the food staple for many developing countries, which rely on shark meat as their source of protein. When the shark finners throw the dying sharks back into the ocean, up to 95% of the shark is discarded. This is valuable protein being wasted.

Each country with a coastline is responsible for laws and regulations related to fishing in its waters. Some countries have shark-finning legislation and many stipulate that fins must arrive in a 5% weight ratio of the shark carcasses onboard. Very few countries demand that sharks arrive in port with fins attached.

DID YOU KNOW? Over 8,000 tons of shark fins are processed each year[10].

There are fears that some species will be threatened if shark finning isn't controlled better. The United Nations Convention on the Trade of Endangered Species of Flora and Fauna (CITES) lists the whale, basking and great white shark as species that could become threatened if trade is not controlled. So far, 169 countries have agreed to be legally bound by CITES.

Finning is illegal in several countries, and while banning the practice of finning is a start, it's not the whole solution. Finning bans are difficult to enforce, especially on the high seas.

A ban on the trade of fins, prohibiting the possession, sale, offering for sale or distribution of shark fins or products, is a complementary part of the solution. Trade bans have simplified and reduced the cost of enforcement.

Shark sanctuaries, where sharks are fully protected by strong laws and enforcement with the support and cooperation of local communities, is the third part of the solution. Sanctuaries produce tangible economic benefits to local populations with marine tourism, and can be found in Raja Ampat, Indonesia, the Marshall Islands, the Bahamas and Palau.

Many coastal populations make money from ecotourism, using sharks to encourage visitors. An estimate for hammerhead sharks suggests that a live shark, over the course of its lifetime, is worth $1.6 million in ecotourism. The dead shark brings in only $200. The University of British Colombia predicts that shark ecotourism will be worth more than the global shark fisheries in just a few years.

 DID YOU KNOW? Sharks have inhabited the planet for more than 400 million years[13].

China (the main consumer of shark fins) is working towards ending shark finning. The Chinese government began prohibiting the serving of shark fin soup at official banquets in 2012. While this is a great step forwards, plenty of high-end restaurants still serve shark fin soup at anywhere between US$50 and US$400 per serving.

There is no scientific evidence that culling sharks will lead to a decrease in shark attacks and increase ocean safety. To eliminate shark culling, we need education to increase public awareness of the need to coexist safely with sharks. Non-lethal bather protection programmes can be increased, such as aerial and coastal surveillance, shark barriers and sonar trials. Aerial spotting with helicopters and light planes works effectively for popular beaches. Using social media, sharks can 'tweet' their location as they swim past underwater detectors.

Protecting sharks is a difficult job, more difficult than protecting dolphins or seals. The popular view in the media is that seals are cute and dolphins have a cheeky smile, while sharks have sharp teeth and look menacing.

 **DID YOU KNOW?** Fishermen kill and cut up dolphins for shark bait for their long-line hooks.

Perhaps the best way of protecting the sharks is to change public opinion.

The largest shark is the whale shark, which has been known to get as big as 18 metres in length, and the second biggest is the basking shark that can grow up to 8m. Both of these gentle giants are plankton eaters.

In the ray family, the biggest is the oceanic manta, which can grow to a disc size of up to 7m, with a weight of about 1,350kg. Manta (and mobula) rays have the largest brains of all 32,000 species (approximately) of fish known to date and they are also plankton eaters.

WHAT'S HAPPENING WITH THE RAYS?

Manta and mobula rays are large filter-feeding animals. Their flesh is considered relatively poor quality by humans all around the world, meaning they haven't been targeted by fisheries. Until now.

> Mantas can be found along productive coastlines with regular upwelling (where wind-driven movement of dense, cooler, and usually nutrient-rich water is driven towards the ocean surface), in oceanic island groups and near offshore pinnacles and seamounts.
>
> Mantas are threatened by targeted fishing and bycatch.
>
> They are caught throughout their global warm water range in the Atlantic, Pacific and Indian Ocean in commercial and artisanal fisheries.

Recently, manta rays and their close relatives have become a more desirable product as they are the latest commodity in the environmentally destructive Chinese medicinal trade, making them a target for fishermen around the world.

The mantas and mobula rays are beautiful, complex creatures with gill plates: thin cartilage filaments that enable them to filter plankton out of the water. They have five pairs of gills, each protected inside a gill slit. Inside each of the ten gill slits there is one gill plate forming a circle around the periphery of the slit, trapping the planktonic food as it's funnelled through the ray's mouth.

 DID YOU KNOW? Manta rays are large animals with few natural predators.

The gill plates, when dried, are the most valuable parts of the rays. In India, Sri Lanka and Indonesia there are increasingly large fisheries. The plates are just a tiny percentage of a manta or mobula's body mass, yet they sell for significantly more than the rest of the body parts put together.

Plastic contains toxins, and when it's in the ocean it absorbs more toxins. Plastics entangle and kill sea life, and they don't biodegrade.

 DID YOU KNOW? Approximately 10–20 million tons of plastic end up in the oceans each year[19].

Plastic is made from petroleum and natural gas liquids. The annual plastic production and usage grew from 1.5 million tons in 1950 to 230 million tons in 2009. Plastic products tend to be single use, meaning after we've used them we throw them away.

 DID YOU KNOW? A recent study conservatively estimated that 5.25 trillion plastic particles weighing a total of 268,940 tons are currently floating in the world's oceans[20].

Around the world's oceans are 'garbage islands'. These islands are formed by large systems of moving ocean currents, known as 'ocean gyres', where water is constantly circulating like a vortex. Plastic in the ocean is drawn to the middle of these gyres. Over time it breaks down into small particles of just a few millimetres, but because it is not biodegradable, it doesn't disappear. Thus, as more and more plastic accumulates, it forms into giant garbage islands.

There are five major gyres and many smaller tropical, sub-tropical and polar gyres. The five major ones are the[21]:

INDIAN OCEAN GYRE. Home to one of the most recently discovered garbage islands (in 2010), this is at least five million km². According to the team who discovered it, it takes the patch six years to do a full rotation, alternatively hitting the coasts of Africa and Australia on its way.

acidity of the oceans, making it difficult for marine organisms to thrive, especially those that build shells or skeletons.

 DID YOU KNOW? 18% of greenhouse gas emissions come from animal farms[36].

Fertiliser run-off creates eutrophication, which causes a dense growth of plant life and algal bloom – a rapid increase or accumulation in the population of algae in aquatic systems. This depletes the oxygen content in the water, and that affects marine life. Pesticides and other chemical substances used to kill animals or insects that threaten crops are all sources of pollution, too. These chemicals are essentially poisons. When rain falls on the crops, many of these poisons are swept away into rivers and streams that eventually make their way to the ocean, where they are a threat to marine life.

Toxic metals from industrial contamination can destroy the biochemistry, behaviour, reproduction and growth in marine life.

 DID YOU KNOW? 80% of pollution to the marine environment comes from the land[37].

Chemicals from industry and mining activities can enter the ocean. They seep through soil, drain off the land, or enter the water during either their manufacture, use or from accidental leaks.

Until the 1970s chemicals and rubbish were deliberately dumped into the oceans. It became common practice to dispose of pesticides and radioactive waste, assuming that it would get dissolved to safe levels. Storing radioactive waste at the bottom of the oceans is a bad strategy. It is harmful to both the organisms that inhabit the ocean and humans. It's also a very expensive process.

DID YOU KNOW? Russia is the biggest contributor to nuclear and radioactive waste dumping in the oceans[38].

Russia stores a vast amount of radioactive material in the ocean in poor containment facilities, with the obvious risk of leaks. Radiation can destroy entire ecosystems and contaminate the whole food chain.

DID YOU KNOW? Radioactive waste from the Fukushima Daiichi nuclear power plant in Japan has slowly been leaking into the ocean from a drainage ditch[39].

Poor insulation of containers, volcanic activity and tectonic plate movement may cause radiation to leak out into the oceans, where it can be carried by currents. Because the earth is constantly shifting, scientists have discovered that previous sites approved for ocean dumping are now not so safe[40].

HOW CAN WE COMBAT OCEAN POLLUTION?

Use less plastic and recycle. While plastic can take a million years to break down, recycled plastic can be made into new bottles, carpeting and even clothing.

DID YOU KNOW? There are 3.2 billion kg of non-recyclable plastic produced every year[41].

Choose safer plastics. There are many types of plastics used in everyday life, with varying effects on the environment and your health. Knowing your plastics is a good first step in reducing their overall use and therefore their negative effects.

> They are two types of plastic: thermoplastics, which can be re-moulded into new shapes easily through high temperature, and thermosetting, which is very rigid and has more resistance to heat.
>
> They both display a negative impact on the environment, so we need to avoid excessive use of plastic materials.

Reduce plastic in the waste. Improve solid waste management and increase capture and reuse.

Eat less meat and dairy to reduce the effects of extensive animal farming, and always eat local sustainably raised meat and dairy.

It's not easy to replace the pesticide system, but with proper research and management it is possible to use less of these harmful chemicals. Farmers are encouraged to control their irrigation systems carefully to minimise their use of fresh water.

Governments need to pass legislation and approve new sites for dumping of toxic and nuclear waste, and to find ways of removing containers currently stored in danger areas. There are only a few 'safe zones' for storing nuclear waste, and getting to those places is very expensive.

The idea of the 'circular economy' is gaining ground (see the Ellen MacArthur information in the chapter entitled 'So What Can We Do?'). There is broad agreement that industry needs to move towards products that maximise recycling and re-use.

We do need to consider, from the very beginning,
the second, third and, indeed, fourth life of
the products we use in everyday life.

✳ HRH CHARLES, PRINCE OF WALES ✳

Most companies work to a linear economy, which is a 'take, make, dispose' model of production, meaning your mobile phone is designed to be thrown away when you're tired of it. The circular economy, on the other hand, promotes reducing waste and avoiding pollution by design, in other words, planning to reuse and recycle products and by-products of the manufacturing process. Many big companies, like Phillips, Dell and Energizer, are already making strides.

Companies like SodaStream are taking a pop at the bottled water and canned beverages industry. In 2013, SodaStream was unable to run its advert during the Super Bowl. The ad claimed that: 'With SodaStream, we could have saved 500 million bottles on game day alone', but the network CBS rejected the ad because it hit out at other big advertisers like Coca-Cola and Pepsi. SodaStream's CEO Daniel Birnbaum knows that plastic bottles cause untold damage to the environment, and the ad showed that there is a more eco-friendly alternative.

WHAT YOU CAN DO

Get rid of your own rubbish carefully. Recycle, reuse and refuse – sort and separate items into the correct recycling bins; reuse plastic bags, bottles and packaging; and stop over-consuming. Ask companies to reduce packaging and create ocean friendly materials.

DID YOU KNOW? The average American throws away approximately 83 kg (185 pounds) of plastic per year[42].

Drink tap water, if it's safe in your area. Don't use plastic bags, straws, food containers or cups.

Avoid products containing micro-plastics – have a look at www.beatthemicrobead.org for products to avoid.

Spread the word. When you see people throwing away plastic bags or using bottled water, tell them about the sea turtles. Explain about the garbage patches circulating around the world.

Take your unused and unwanted prescription and non-prescription drugs to participating pharmacies, who place them into secure bins and send them off to be incinerated. In some cases the incineration process even creates energy that is used to power homes and businesses.

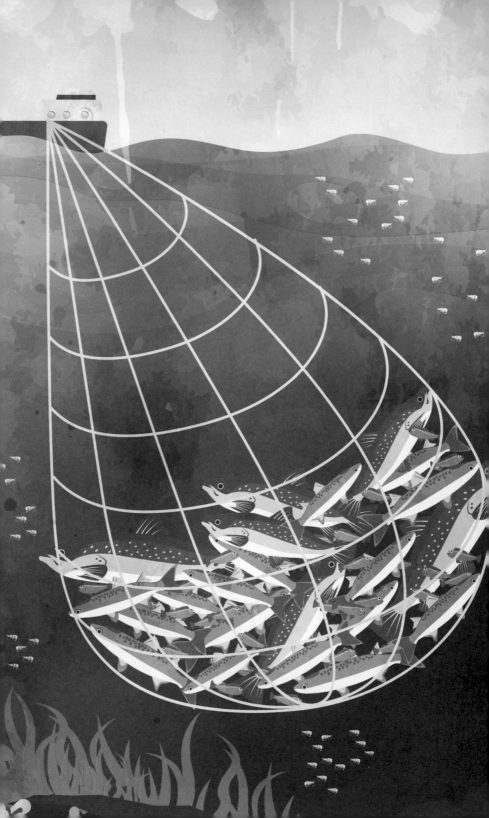

UNSUSTAINABLE FISHING

The big fish, the bill fish, the groupers, the big things will be gone. It is happening now. If things go unchecked, we'll have a sea full of little horrible things that nobody wants to eat. We might end up with a marine junkyard dominated by plankton.

✳ DR DANIEL PAULY, PROFESSOR AND DIRECTOR OF THE UNIVERSITY OF BRITISH COLUMBIA'S FISHERIES CENTRE ✳

WHAT'S HAPPENING? Catching more fish than the system can support leads to a steady degradation to the entire system. Overfishing is not sustainable. Our oceans are being plundered.

Atlantic bluefin tuna spawn just once a year and do not reach maturity until they are eight to twelve years old. The bluefin tuna is estimated to have declined at least 51% over the past three generations (around thirty-nine years) and is listed as endangered.

People are taking far more fish out of the ocean than can be replaced by those fish remaining. Most of the top ten marine fisheries, accounting for about 30% of all capture fisheries' production, are fully exploited or overexploited[43].

 DID YOU KNOW? Over 32% of all the world's fish stocks are either overexploited or depleted[44].

Several important commercial fish populations have declined to the point where their survival is threatened. And it's not just the fish we eat

world's catch is discarded due to inappropriate fish sizes, or simply due to unintended by-catch.

DID YOU KNOW? By-catch occurs because the nets trap everything larger than the net's mesh, which includes juvenile fish, sharks, seabirds, marine turtles and cetaceans (whales, dolphins, porpoises)[49].

Despite new technologies, by-catch is still a major problem. It causes avoidable deaths and injuries, and the fishing methods can be harmful to the marine environments where they are employed.

DID YOU KNOW? Incidental capture of turtles by longlines, trawls and gillnets is the single greatest threat to the survival of most populations.

Poor fisheries management in some countries contributes to the problem. Pirate fishing ignores regulations on net mesh sizes, quotas, permitted fishing areas and other by-catch mitigation measures.

WHY IS OVER-FISHING A PROBLEM?

The most obvious impact of overfishing is that there will be no more fish for humans. If we do not act quickly and decisively, this will happen in our lifetimes. But there is far more to this than lack of fish for our supper.

DID YOU KNOW? Three point one billion people depend on fish as an important part of their diet[50].

The impacts of declining fish catches are being felt painfully by many coastal fishing communities around the world. People in Newfoundland, Canada thought the cod stocks of the Grand Banks were inexhaustible. But in 1992 the cod fishery collapsed and around 40,000 people lost their jobs almost overnight, including 10,000 fishermen. The cod have still not recovered. Science indicates that the ecosystem has substantially changed, meaning that the cod may never make a comeback.

 DID YOU KNOW? Oceans support the livelihoods of an estimated 520 million people who rely on fishing and fishing related activities[51].

Illegal fishing causes assumptions that fewer fish are being caught than is in fact the case. This means experts overestimate the size of the stock and set the following year's catch quotas too high, potentially accelerating the overexploitation of the stock.

According to marine ecologists, unsustainable fishing is the greatest threat to ocean ecosystems. It destroys the physical environments of marine life, and distorts the entire food chain. If the food chain breaks, the consequences ripple up and down to all the living organisms in the chain.

Constantly fishing for particular species, like the bluefin tuna (which is many people's favourite), means that soon that kind of fish will be extinct. All three species of bluefin tuna are threatened and have reached population levels from which recovery is practically impossible.

 DID YOU KNOW? Five out of the eight tuna species are at risk of extinction[52].

It's estimated that over 300,000 small whales, dolphins and porpoises die from entanglement in fishing nets each year. This is the largest cause of mortality for small cetaceans. Species such as the vaquita and Māui's dolphin face extinction if non-selective fishing gear is not eliminated. Hundreds of thousands of endangered loggerhead turtles and critically endangered leatherback turtles drown annually on longlines set for tuna and swordfish.

Many large fisheries stay for months in deep seas and sometimes lose their nets. These nets remain for many decades, continuing to trap and catch fish and end up killing them, causing unknown levels of destruction.

 DID YOU KNOW? Three hundred thousand dolphins and porpoises die each year as a result of becoming entangled in discarded fishing nets, among other items.

The effects of blast fishing can be horrifying. The water can be littered with dead or struggling fish because only a portion of the fish that are killed are retrieved and many sink to the bottom.

 DID YOU KNOW? Over 65% of the world's seagrass communities have been lost by land reclamation, eutrophication, disease and unsustainable fishing practices[53].

In addition to the overfishing itself, imagine the pollution caused every day by the thousands of trawlers and fishing vessels used worldwide. Water pollution from spills, the environmental impact from items 'lost' overboard, and the physical impact on the seabed from bottom trawling all have devastating consequences for marine ecosystems.

the seal using a hakapik or other club of a type that is sanctioned by the governing authority[57].

TURTLES END UP AS BY-CATCH. Sea turtles, although reptiles, regularly suffer a similar fate as their marine mammal cousins. They breathe air, they inhabit similar locations, and they regularly appear as by-catch. They are one of the longest-living animals in the ocean, and yet every year hundreds of thousands of them are accidentally caught and die in shrimp nets and other fishing gear. Endangered loggerheads, green turtles and leatherbacks are especially vulnerable.

DID YOU KNOW? Fossil records show that turtles appeared during the Triassic period and were around with dinosaurs in the Jurassic period.

Sea turtle by-catch is a worldwide problem. The National Marine Fisheries Service has estimated that 500,000 loggerhead, green, leatherback, hawksbill and Kemp's ridley sea turtles, all listed as threatened or endangered under the Endangered Species Act, are injured in some way each year by shrimp fishing gear.

DID YOU KNOW? All seven species of marine turtles are currently listed as threatened or endangered[58].

DOLPHINS, WHALES AND ORCAS (KILLER WHALES) ARE UNDER THREAT. Dolphins, whales and orcas face two types of threat: natural dangers in their habitat and dangers from human activities. Natural dangers happen for any wild animals, and do not represent great danger to their population unless it is an epidemic.

DID YOU KNOW? Sperm whales can dive for over an hour to depths over 1,000m (3,280ft).

The list of threats to dolphins, whales and orcas from human activities is comprehensive:

COMMERCIAL HUNTING. They are killed for their fat, skin, flesh and internal organs. They are still hunted in Japan, Greenland, Indonesia and some parts of the Caribbean.

 DID YOU KNOW? More than 14,000 whales have been killed in Japan since the commercial whale-hunting ban in 1986[59].

CAPTURED FOR ENTERTAINMENT. Orcas and dolphins are very intelligent, which makes them attractive to humans, who teach them to perform tricks and display them in aquariums.

HABITAT POLLUTION. Oil spills, for example, are dangerous, both directly in the form of physical effects on the body and indirectly through decreased prey.

EXCESSIVE NOISE. Dolphins and whales are sensitive since they use echolocation, so military and industrial activities that generate excessive noise can cause problems for them.

DECREASED PREY due to habitat pollution and overfishing.

 DID YOU KNOW? The pilot whale can dive to 500m when hunting for food and eats squid, fish and octopus.

COLLISIONS WITH BOATS. A crash with any vessel can lead to wounds that have the potential to get infected and cause death.

CONFRONTATIONS WITH FISHERMEN. Some see the orcas as a threat because they have learned to steal fish.

 DID YOU KNOW? The killer whale or orca is a toothed whale, and is the largest member of the dolphin family.

CLIMATE CHANGE. Changes in temperature or water level of the oceans can reduce the availability of food, demanding changes in behaviour and causing starvation.

Whales and dolphins play an important role in stabilising the aquatic food chain and the reproduction of other species. When more are killed, the ecosystem is destabilised, causing changes in the food supply for other types of marine animals. Their excrement also helps stabilise the offset of carbon in the atmosphere, creating a healthier environment for land and aquatic life forms[60].

 DID YOU KNOW? A blue whale can consume 40 million krill per day.

Without the whale species, the entire world's economy would see a huge negative shift. Whale and dolphin watching brings in billions of dollars and helps stimulate economic growth. No whales, no whale watching. No dolphins, no swimming with dolphins.

VAQUITA (PORPOISE) AND TOTOABA AND ILLEGAL GILLNET FISH-ING. Just fifty years ago, the critically endangered vaquita was discovered around Mexico's Upper Gulf of California. They reach a maximum length of about 1 metre, and are the smallest of the porpoise family.

In the spring of 2016, three vaquitas were found dead, all from the same problem: entanglement in nets. These shy animals easily get entangled in fishing gear, particularly gillnets set to catch shrimp, sharks and other finfish.

 DID YOU KNOW? In the twenty years to 2016 the population of Vaquitas declined from 600 to less than 60[61].

Illegal gillnet fishing for totoaba, a large schooling marine fish, which can grow up to 1.8 metres in length and is also found only in the Gulf of California, has made them critically endangered. Although totoaba fishing has been banned in Mexico since 1975, a black market exists for their swim bladders, which are used to make soup and unproven traditional medicine treatments.

Mexico announced a two-year ban on most gillnets in the northern Gulf of California, and an increase in enforcement action against the illegal totoaba fisheries. However, illegal fishing still occurs at night. In order to avoid the few enforcement authorities that are policing the waters, illegal fishers often dump or abandon their nets, creating 'ghost nets' that catch and kill all sorts of marine life.

 DID YOU KNOW? The vaquita is the most endangered marine mammal in the world.

In 2015 only sixty vaquitas were reported in the Gulf of California. Their numbers are still falling.

WHY IS MARINE MAMMAL ERADICATION A PROBLEM?

When it comes to survival and the food chain, marine mammals play a large and important role in maintaining a healthy marine ecosystem. Around 20–30% of marine mammals are endangered or threatened and their loss will impact aquatic life.

The food chain is complex and subtle, sometimes considered a 'food web' due to its intricacies and multiple connections. While the notion that the 'big fish eat the smaller fish' has some validity, it isn't the whole picture. It is difficult to predict what effect the decline or elimination of one species will have on the whole ecosystem.

Organisms are grouped in the food pyramid by the roles they play in the food chain. The base of the pyramid is made up of producers, such as phytoplankton and seaweed, followed by the herbivores, then the carnivores. At each level, the consumer species enjoy about 10% of the energy they consume from the level below – in other words, when a shark eats a squid it will get 10% of its energy value. The rest is lost as waste and energy consumed in movement and heat. Each level supports a smaller number of organisms, and a top-level consumer, such as a shark, is supported by millions of primary producers at the base of the food web.

The marine mammals are near the top of the food chain. The elimination of one species could decrease the chances of survival for other species, especially those that rely on the eliminated species' prey for survival. If a prey species were to become extinct, then its predators also face the possibility of extinction. If a predator were to become extinct, its prey could overpopulate and quickly consume its food supply, leading to future starvation.

For example, sea otters have a limiting effect on sea urchins, one of their favourite foods. If the sea otter reduces in numbers, the sea urchins may increase. Sea urchins eat kelp. Kelp provides a home for small and young

To save the vaquita, the Mexican government must commit financing, staff and political will to ensure that a complete gillnet ban is fully and diligently enforced.

WHAT YOU CAN DO

Join organisations such as Sea Shepherd, Greenpeace, Shark Guardian and WNF.

Only consume fish from sustainable fisheries. Companies include MSC, ASC and Friends of the Sea products.

Read the section on pollution for more ideas.

MARINE HABITAT DESTRUCTION

You are not a drop in the ocean.
You are the entire ocean in a drop.

✳ RUMI ✳

Marine habitats are home to seaweeds, marine algae, seagrasses and mangroves, and include estuaries, swamps, marshes and wetlands. These are critical areas for the whole marine ecosystem, as they serve as breeding grounds or nurseries for countless marine species. As we noted earlier, climate and sea changes, ocean temperature rises, a reduction in the solubility of oxygen in the water, and pollution are all taking their toll on marine habitats.

DID YOU KNOW? The Intergovernmental Panel on Climate Change predicts a rise of between 1.4°C and 5.8°C in global temperatures by the end of the century[64].

WHAT'S HAPPENING?

Marine habitat destruction and loss is where the marine environment or the ecological set-up is unable to support life due to degradation. This is a process that is caused by various natural and human activities such as destructive fishing activities like bottom trawling and dynamiting coral reefs, and coastal development when marshes are dredged to make way for housing developments.

 DID YOU KNOW? Land plants only produce about one-third of the oxygen we breathe. The rest comes from the ocean.

THE CORALS AND CORAL REEFS ARE BEING BLEACHED AND DESTROYED. Coral bleaches when the water is too warm for too long, as the coral polyps get stressed and spit out the algae that live inside them. Without the algae, the coral flesh becomes transparent, revealing the white skeleton beneath. The algae provide the coral with 90% of its energy, so without them the coral begins to starve. The coral dies and gets taken over by a blanket of seaweed unless the temperatures quickly return to normal.

 DID YOU KNOW? We've lost between 25 and 40% of the world's corals[65].

Once the coral has been taken over, it can take decades to recover, if it's lucky and not hit by other stressors such as water pollution. Corals are highly tuned in to their environmental surroundings – when something in their environment happens, they know about it. If the stresses persist, the corals will die.

Bleaching affects the majority of the tropical reefs around the world, with a large proportion dying. The rate of recovery is different from region to region and depends on the health of the reef[66]. Waves and storms break dead coral skeletons down into coral rubble, leading to a change in the whole ecosystem, and often thick seaweed takes over, blocking fish that can no longer use the coral as shelter. This is ecosystem destruction in action.

HOW CAN WE COMBAT MARINE HABITAT DESTRUCTION?

We need to maintain and improve the biodiversity of the marine habitat, and in turn protect the services these habitats provide for humans and other ecosystems.

There is no international legislation for seagrasses, so protection occurs by local and regional agencies. To help seagrasses we must limit damage such as excessive trawling and dredging, run-off pollution and harmful fishing practices like dynamite or cyanide fishing.

To combat the environmental threat, we must control pollution. We need environmental conservation bodies to help the various governments draw up laws to control industrialisation and waste disposal.

As we discussed previously, control or moderation of fishing activities to make them sustainable will help. Overfishing damages the aquatic ecology and food chain. Fishing must be done in such a way that plants and animals are not rendered extinct in the process. We need to educate people that respecting and treating the ocean and plants with care will be to everyone's benefit, in both the medium and long term.

Governments must limit the spread of urbanisation and coastal developments that pose serious threat to the marine habitat and commit to the goals of the Paris Agreement. We must enforce strict use of designated shipping routes to limit damage caused by ocean transport, and reduce the risk of oil spills and other unnatural disasters.

these NGOs arose out of political decisions and are still, to a large degree, politically and economically driven.

Charities have a mission to work for a social good as torchbearers for human rights, the environment or social development. Even they are subverted, though, with monies donated being channelled away and not reaching their intended destinations.

Big businesses have to meet shareholder expectations, and saving the sharks isn't usually part of their five-year business plan.

WHY DON'T WE FIX THE PROBLEMS?

When life gets you down, you know what you gotta do?
Just keep swimming.

✳ DORY, *FINDING NEMO* ✳

There are probably five reasons why we, as individuals, aren't making a difference:

APATHY. There's always something else to do. We think it's someone else's problem, or something we can fix tomorrow.

LACK OF TIME. We are busier now than ever before, with families, school, work, and leisure all using up our precious minutes. There are Facebook posts to like, Snapchat photos to take, television series to watch, YouTube, Twitter and Instagram – distractions all vying for our attention.

WE DON'T BELIEVE WE CAN MAKE A DIFFERENCE. Possibly the most worrying is when we truly don't believe that what we do will make a difference. We think that we are too small and insignificant; that no one will listen to us.

IT'S ALREADY TOO LATE. Some people, including scientists, think it's too late – that what we do now won't make a difference.

WE DON'T KNOW WHAT TO DO. Maybe the biggest problem is that people don't know what to do, how to do it and with whom.

I know I suffered from these five problems when I was busy working, bringing up my kids, racing from appointment to appointment. I always believed I'd do something to save the oceans, but not today. Maybe tomorrow, when I had more time. I wasn't sure I could make a difference, and I really didn't know what I could do, but it was there in the back of my mind.

Then I realised that I was part of the problem. I used plastics, drove a car, ate fish, flushed the toilet. I knew that my day-to-day life was contributing to breaking the ecosystem. But it's always a challenge for the people who broke the thing to fix it. The same thinking that got us into this mess won't get us out of it. Sometimes, like now, we need a fresh approach, more energy and a change in attitude to make a difference.

And this is where young people come in.

The Millennials and Generation Z, those between the ages of eight and twenty-eight, need to lead the way. On the whole, they are better with communications, media and digital technologies, and are working, thinking and operating in a totally different way to the generations that came before them. They don't tend to see the same limitations that older people see.

The destruction of the planet is not young people's destiny. The effects of the last few millennia are not irrevocable, and age doesn't matter. With hope and a positive outlook, we can turn tides.

However, there are hundreds of channels vying for young people's attention. I would ask them to disconnect from the distractions and get out to the oceans for a fantastic experience with nature, learn about the real world, the environment, and discover whole new dimensions.

 DID YOU KNOW? 52% of the global population is under 30 years old[75].

Young people are a powerful force. They have the ability to find out any information they need, strength in numbers, and an expected life span longer than any time in history. Current world leaders are nearing the end of their lives, but young people might live another sixty, seventy or eighty years. Together, we have to make significant changes so they can enjoy their long lives in a healthy, sustainable world.

If we create a chain reaction, starting with small projects on a small scale, we can prove our case and get other people, companies, governments interested. I want to start my case in Southeast Asia. I hope to lead with my own small but positive footprints.

WHAT'S THE URGENCY?

I have been impressed with the urgency of doing. Knowing is not enough; we must apply. Being willing is not enough; we must do.

✳ LEONARDO DA VINCI ✳

We need to think about what we put in to the oceans and what we take out of them. This is a balance. When we are out of balance, we break the system.

Turning
TIDES

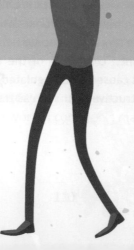

DID YOU KNOW? Trawling is as damaging to the seabed as all other fishing gear combined.

Primary fishing grounds are likely to become increasingly infested by invasive species, many introduced from ship ballast water.

The cumulative impacts of climate change and existing pressures of over-harvesting, bottom trawling, invasive species, coastal development and pollution appear to be concentrated in 10–15% of the oceans, which also happen to be the most important fishing grounds. The effects will be most pronounced for developing countries where fish are an increasingly important and valuable export product.

DID YOU KNOW? Plastic in the ocean could outweigh fish by 2050[85].

Substantial resources need to be allocated to reducing climate and non-climate pressures on the oceans, to build resilience against climate change and to ensure that further collapses in fish stocks are avoided in coming decades. We need actions for a reduction of coastal pollution, establishment of marine protected areas in deeper waters, protection of seamounts and parts of the continental shelves against bottom trawling, and stronger regulation of fisheries.

PUTTING IT INTO PERSPECTIVE

Around 4.55 billion years ago the earth was formed as a consequence of the soup of atoms and molecules caused by the big bang almost 9 billion years previously. The oceans appeared 4.2 billion years ago and it's their formation that created first life. The first marine animals appeared 800 million years ago, and the first sharks 450 million years later, 120 million

SO WHAT CAN WE DO?

We do not need to stop using and enjoying the oceans. However, we must manage our use to ensure their sustainability for the present and for future generations. If you want your kids and your kids' kids to enjoy the breathtaking beauty of the oceans, we all need to act, now.

I used to study and train in Judo ju: the gentle way in Japanese. Judo relies on a few key principles: maximum efficiency with minimum effort, mutual welfare and benefit, and softness controls hardness. In the judo match context this means resisting a more powerful opponent will usually result in your defeat. Adjusting to and evading your opponent's attack will cause them to lose balance, their power will be reduced, and you will defeat them. In other words, it is possible for weaker opponents to beat significantly stronger ones.

You may be feeling that our goal to save the oceans and marine life, and ultimately save ourselves, is too big to achieve. You may feel like your efforts won't make a difference; that things have too far gone. I believe that with your help, we can make a difference.

Let's think about how.

MAXIMUM EFFICIENCY WITH MINIMUM EFFORT

We need to discover the methods and channels for getting the most gain from our efforts, and we can use the very channels that are distracting us and pulling us away from nature to help gain traction. Let's use social networking and media. Set up Facebook groups and share the real stories. Use crowdsourcing to collect supporters and money to fund great ideas. Help the press discover interesting, positive stories about our oceans and the people saving them. Get on television; share the stories of our heroes.

a mission for Moore. He had grown up in Long Beach, California, swimming in Alamitos Bay and sailing to remote places like Guadalupe Island and Hawaii, and had seen first-hand the decline of coastal marine ecosystems.

Prior to Moore's first research voyage in 1999, nobody had conducted an expedition to study plastic marine pollution in the area that has become known as 'The Eastern Garbage Patch'. Since then, Moore has become a world-renowned investigator in this field. He has continued leading sea expeditions, combing through more than 150,000 miles of ocean, and authors scientific papers on plastic particulate pollution.

Moore's 'do-it-yourself' entrepreneurial brand of environmentalism, described in his book *Plastic Ocean*, has brought worldwide attention to the issue. He speaks to audiences across the globe, explaining how plastic debris can be seen as the number one threat to the planet.

Moore has won the 2014 Peter Benchley 'Hero of the Seas' Ocean Award among many others, and has been featured as the Great Pacific Garbage Patch expert on *Nightline*, National Public Radio, *Rolling Stone*, *The Wall Street Journal*, NBC, CBS, CNN and more.

AGAINST PLASTIC OCEANS – Craig Leeson – www.plasticoceans.org. Plastic Oceans is a global network of independent not-for-profits and charitable organisations, united in their aims to change the world's attitude towards plastic within a generation. There are currently four Plastic Oceans Foundation entities: United States, Canada, Hong Kong and United Kingdom, serving both the ocean and the public.

A Plastic Ocean – the film. Producer Jo Ruxton joined an expedition to the Great Pacific Garbage Patch in the North Pacific Gyre, 1,500 miles off the coast of San Francisco, to ascertain its impact. When the expedition discovered free-floating micro-plastics instead of an anticipated solid mass that could be contained, Jo knew she had to begin the film that would become *A Plastic Ocean*.

Jo had worked for the WWF International in Hong Kong and partnered with director and journalist Craig Leeson. Their first collaboration was on a documentary about endangered pink dolphins in Hong Kong, and Jo and Craig brought on board Dr Lindsay Porter, an expert in cetaceans (whales and dolphins). Together they contacted the world's experts to see what was known about plastic pollution in the gyres.

The team expanded to include Dr Bonnie Monteleone who had already found micro-plastic in other gyres she had investigated. She joined the expedition to the South Pacific Gyre. Then, with new information emerging about the extent of the issue in each of the ocean gyres, free diving champion Tanya Streeter joined the team. Together they set off on what would be a four-year global odyssey to explore the issue of plastics in our oceans and its effect on marine ecosystems and human health, including endocrine disruption.

FOR THE CORALS – Richard Vevers – **www.theoceanagency.org.** Richard Vevers was an advertising executive and is now the chief executive of The Ocean Agency, a not-for-profit company he founded to raise awareness of environmental problems.

When he realised the scale of the destruction facing the oceans, he decided to combine his thirty-year diving hobby and his work to build The Ocean Agency. He was mostly concerned about coral bleaching, caused by climate change. Now he travels the world, documenting dead and dying coral reefs.

AGAINST POLLUTION – Dame Ellen MacArthur – **www.ellenmacarthur foundation.org.** When she was only twenty-eight, in 2005, yachtswoman Ellen MacArthur achieved the fastest single-handed circumnavigation of the globe, sailing more than 26,000 miles in just over seventy-one days. She had to learn to cope with limited supplies of water, food and fuel, and this made Ellen acutely aware of how important her scarce resources were to her survival.

In September 2010, she launched the Ellen MacArthur Foundation, with the goal of 'accelerating the transition to a regenerative circular economy'. Ellen is passionate about moving towards an economic system that retains and reuses resources, which makes environmental and business sense.

Our economy today is linear, driven through taking in material at the ground, making something out of it, and then throwing it away when we no longer need it. A circular economy is designed to be regenerative. For example, we would design a car for re-manufacture, disassembly and de-componentisation, which means the materials in the global economy that currently flow off the end of the conveyor belt can go back in.

There are two types of materials under consideration in the circular economy: biological nutrients designed to re-enter the biosphere safely, and technical nutrients. The technical nutrients (plastics, for example) are designed to circulate at high quality in the production system without entering the biosphere; they should be restorative and regenerative by design.

When companies understand what a circular economy is and set it as their goal, every decision they make within their businesses takes us one step closer to it.

Ellen is also a founder of the Ellen MacArthur Cancer Trust, set up in 2003: a charity which takes young people aged between eight and twenty-four sailing to help them regain their confidence on their way to recovery from cancer, leukaemia and other serious illnesses. Ellen received a knighthood for her work in 2005.

Find out more: https://www.ellenmacarthurfoundation.org.

Margo Peyton, Scuba Mom, Founder of Kids Sea Camp, Cross Generation Diving Experiences – http://familydivers.com. Margo Peyton is a creator and a visionary who has worked hard to support family values

TOGETHER WE CAN TURN TIDES

A MANIFESTO TO SAVE THE OCEANS, PLANET & OURSELVES

THE ORCA GENTLE WAY

Open Your Eyes, Mind and Heart to the problems
Take **R**esponsibility, not blame
Make a **C**ommitment to making a difference
Take **A**ction right now…

harmful dioxins into the atmosphere. Sisters Melati and Isabel Wijsen, just fifteen and thirteen years old, plan to stop plastic bags from ruining their beautiful island home. They have done a TED talk and beach clean-ups, and have finally convinced their governor to commit to a plastic bag-free Bali by 2018.

Don't ever let anyone tell you that you're too young or you won't understand. We're not telling you it's going to be easy. We're telling you it's going to be worth it.

* ISABEL WIJSEN *

In 2013, the girls set up a youth-driven social initiative at www.byebye plasticbags.org to encourage youngsters to get the people of Bali to say no to plastic bags. They were inspired to action by a lesson in class about significant people like Nelson Mandela, Princess Diana and Mahatma Ghandi. Instead of going home and forgetting that important lesson, they wondered what they could do right now. Bye Bye Plastic Bags now has a volunteer team of twenty-five to thirty students from all the schools around Bali, local and international.

They created a twenty-five-page booklet in Bahasa Indonesian, illus-trated by one of the local team members (aged thirteen), all about waste management, marine debris and youth empowerment. They're working with the government to get this booklet implemented into all the school systems in Bali, and then hopefully Indonesia.

They started a campaign to 'sticker' the shops, restaurants, hotels, etc. that are plastic bag free to indicate that they are part of the 'One Island, One Voice – Plastic Bag Free Zone'. Every business that gets the sticker will get publicity on the sisters' social media platforms. They also run a pilot village called Pererenan, home to 800 local families. Every Saturday they distribute alternative bags to the local shops and warungs.

They now have young people from every corner of the world reaching out to them to make their own town, village or country plastic bag-free. Bye Bye Plastic Bags can be found in Australia, Jakarta, Guadalajara, New York, Nepal, Myanmar, China, Singapore, and the Philippines.

Follow the sisters on https://www.facebook.com/byebyeplasticbags.

NEVER TOO YOUNG TO GET INVOLVED

Meet Ryan, a recycling hero at three years old (http://ryansrecycling.com). In 2012, Ryan went with his dad to the local recycling centre to cash in a few small bags of cans and bottles. That was when he decided that recycling was in his future. The next day, Ryan told his parents that he wanted to give empty plastic bags to all the neighbours so they could save their recyclables for him. The neighbours did, and so did their friends, and now, Ryan has customers all over Orange County in the USA.

In December 2016 and January 2017, Ryan's recycling story went viral and he was featured on hundreds of websites and radio stations around the world. He appeared on the *Ellen DeGeneres Show*, was featured on ABC *World News* and hundreds of ABC affiliate news stations.

But Ryan hasn't let the fame go to his head. He still spends hours each week sorting through the recyclables, collecting plastic, glass and aluminium, and taking them by the truckload (with a little help from his parents) to the local redemption centre. Ryan is saving the money he collects for his future college education.

Ryan's passion for recycling is making a difference to the amount of recyclable beverage containers that aren't going to the landfill. Those containers also aren't making it to oceans, where they could harm animals and the environment.

directly with students, police stations and pharmacies to dispose of unwanted or unused prescription medication.

The idea for the project came when Baylee's mum, Jodee, asked her dad, Paul, what she should do with some unused pharmaceuticals in their medicine cabinet. Paul posed the question to his Ecology students at Pontiac Township High School, who got stuck in to searching for information from the internet. They got help from local officials from the water company, the police department and the Mayor of Pontiac, Scott McCoy, and uncovered startling information about the effect of pharmaceuticals on the quality of drinking water around the world.

The Ecology students put together presentations for their local pharmacies, like K-mart, Sartoris Super Drugs and Walgreens, asking them to allow patrons to bring in unused prescription drugs for proper and safe disposal. The group has held a letter-writing campaign to ask federal, state and local officials to help educate everyone about the benefits of proper disposal of their prescription and non-prescription drugs, and they're having an effect on legislators, environmental groups and educators.

These students are changing the world. The P2D2 Program is a collaborative effort between students, communities, local pharmacies, police departments, hospitals, city officials and anyone who wants to help. It aims to educate the public about the harm done to the environment, and the misuse and abuse of pharmaceuticals due to the current prescription and non-prescription drug disposal practices worldwide. By providing communities with a proper method of pharmaceutical disposal, it aims to reduce the misuse and abuse of pharmaceuticals, as well as maintaining the quality of water and wildlife for future generations.

The United Nations Environmental Program declared this the number one student environmental programme in the United States and the third best programme in the world in 2012. Now, the students have expanded the P2D2 Program to twenty-seven US states, Turkey, Brazil and Paraguay. In 2013, Baylee was asked to be a keynote speaker at the United Nations Tunza International Youth Conference in Nairobi, Kenya to discuss steps youth can take towards water conservation.

Baylee is a guest writer for the United Nations' *Tunza Youth* magazine and *ARKive* magazine, which documents the endangered species of our world. She's the co-author of an informational student publication on biodiversity for the United Nations. In April of 2014, Baylee was the keynote speaker on water preservation and the P2D2 Program at the International Science and Arts Festival in Istanbul, Turkey.

Help Baylee and the P2D2 Program here: https://p2d2program.wordpress.com.

WHAT MAKES YOU SPECIAL?

You can see from these short case studies and the lives of our ocean heroes that it's people like you who are taking action. Whether you're eight, twenty-eight or eighty-eight, you can make a difference. It doesn't matter where in the world you are, nor your education or background. If you have a strong desire to help the oceans, with the right support you can do it.

I think that there are five positive traits people need to make a difference to our oceans. They are courage, discipline, teamwork, leadership and self-belief.

First of all you need the courage to stand up and be different. It's easy to go along with the flow, following what everyone else is doing. You might need the courage to tell your friends and family that you want to do things differently in the future; that you want to recycle your waste more effectively or stop drinking water from plastic bottles. Some people might think you're crazy or weird. You need the courage and conviction that you can make a difference.

You'll need discipline. Even Ryan, the mini recycling hero with all his recent fame, still sorts through the recycling every week. You'll need to follow through, even if it gets a little difficult.

All of our ocean heroes had help. They knew they couldn't do this alone, so collected teams around them to help them achieve their goals. So, how do you create your team? How can you be a part of something bigger, where the skills and resources are available to help you achieve your goals?

Sometimes you'll need to step up and be the leader, show others the way. Whether you're talking to government policy makers or fishermen, you'll need to lead the discussion, set the course and define the agenda. Our Ocean Ambassador programme will help you develop and hone those skills.

Finally, you'll need to believe in yourself, so you can speak for those who don't have a voice.

THE ORCA GENTLE WAY

Open your eyes, mind and heart to the problems. With open eyes and minds, you can see what's happening right now.

Take Responsibility, not blame. It's easy to blame the fishermen, the cruise ships or the governments for the problems our oceans face. Laying blame at the feet of our ancestors, giant corporations and supermarket chains may be a great conversation starter, but is it really their fault? We are the consumers, the users and polluters, just as they are. We can take responsibility – that means we are able to respond. It's our response, not laying blame, that will enable us to make a difference for all the stakeholders.

TOGETHER WE
CAN TURN TIDES

A MANIFESTO TO SAVE THE OCEANS,
PLANET & OURSELVES

THE ORCA GENTLE WAY

Open Your Eyes, Mind and Heart to the problems
Take **R**esponsibility, not blame
Make a **C**ommitment to making a difference
Take **A**ction right now...

CREATING POSITIVE FOOTPRINTS

Using today's media channels and platforms, we want to spread the word on our programmes and methodology and actively look for partnerships around the globe with like-minded operations, giving them a head start. Through the international school network, we will connect with other regions and continents and work on exchange projects, enabling children from around the globe to join the Ocean Ambassador pool.

THE OCEAN MANIFESTO

HOW CAN YOU MAKE A DIFFERENCE NOW?

I knew that if I failed I wouldn't regret that, but I knew the one thing I might regret is not trying.

* JEFF BEZOS, AMAZON CEO *

In this book, we have covered some of the big problems our oceans face, and stories of people who are making a difference. I am looking for brave adventurers, strong-minded people, leaders and action takers. I'm asking you to get involved, to help save the oceans and the planet, to make your voice heard.

So, what am I asking you to do? From the smallest and simplest tasks, right up to becoming an Ocean Ambassador, I know there is a route for you.

First of all, thanks for buying this book. By educating yourself, you can educate others. You could also watch some of the videos I've mentioned in the book and on our website. And, you are very welcome to come and dive with us. Those first moments underwater will always stay with you.

You might want to connect with us and tell us what you think. Join our Facebook group (facebook.com/orcascuba) to meet like-minded people and share stories and ideas. Why not become an Ocean Ambassador and help me realise my dream? We'd love you to contribute and tell us what you're doing. Show us your photos on our Facebook page or our Instagram account (instagram.com/orcascuba). Identify opportunities to contribute locally; you don't even need to leave the comfort of your own home to make a difference. Also, look for collaborators – we're a team – we need to hear your voice.

Our ORCA Gentle Way asks you to:

Open your eyes, mind and heart to the problems.
Take **R**esponsibility, not blame.
Make a **C**ommitment to making a difference.
Take **A**ction right now.

So, we ask you to commit – decide what you will do today. Will you share the Manifesto? Join a local scuba club? Pick up litter, write to your MP, go on a march?

I was talking to a young intern, Rob, and he reminded me how important it is to define our own versions of success. Before I founded Orca Scuba, I lived a life many people would think was successful. I finally worked out that success isn't defined by wealth or power, but by doing what you love and are passionate about. If I had to give my eighteen-year-old self some advice, looking back with hindsight, I'd say, 'Life will be more fulfilling, and your heart and soul will be inspired by pursuing a career in marine science. Don't get caught up in what society deems as successful; trust your heart instead.'

We are looking for people who are ready to get involved, step up, become a leader, share their heart and passion, and be the voice for the oceans. If you feel excited and inspired to join us, start as an Ocean Ambassador.

Either we succeed together or we fail on our own.

TOGETHER WE CAN TURN TIDES

MANIFESTO TO SAVE THE OCEANS, LANET & OURSELVES

HE ORCA GENTLE WAY

pen Your Eyes, Mind and Heart to the problems

ake **R**esponsibility, not blame

1ake a **C**ommitment to making a difference

ike **A**ction right now...

11 Sharks | Smithsonian Ocean Portal – http://ocean.si.edu/sharks

12 A quarter of sharks and rays threatened with extinction | IUCN – https://www.iucn.org/content/quarter-sharks-and-rays-threatened-extinction

13 Shark Guardian – 100 Awesome Shark Facts – http://www.sharkguardian.org/shark-facts-top-100-shark-guardian

14 WildAid | Mantas – http://www.wildaid.org/mantas

15 The Continuing Threat to Manta and Mobula Rays – 2013-14 Market Surveys, Ghuangzhou, China – SOS & WildAID – IUCN http://cmsdata.iucn.org/downloads/1_the_continuing_threat_to_manta_mobula_rays_2013_14_report_final_july_2_2014_2.pdf

16 Assessing Indonesian manta and devil ray populations through historical landings and fishing community interviews. – Lewis, S.A.;Setiasih, N.;Fahmi, D.;O'Malley, M.P.;Campbell, S.J.;Yusuf, M.;Sianipar, A.B. – https://library.wcs.org/doi/ctl/view/mid/33065/pubid/PUB16070.aspx

17 The Continuing Threat to Manta and Mobula Rays – 2013-14 Market Surveys, Ghuangzhou, China – SOS & WildAID – IUCN http://cmsdata.iucn.org/downloads/1_the_continuing_threat_to_manta_mobula_rays_2013_14_report_final_july_2_2014_2.pdf

18 The Continuing Threat to Manta and Mobula Rays – 2013-14 Market Surveys, Ghuangzhou, China – SOS & WildAID – IUCN http://cmsdata.iucn.org/downloads/1_the_continuing_threat_to_manta_mobula_rays_2013_14_report_final_july_2_2014_2.pdf

19 Global Plastic Production Rises, Recycling Lags | Worldwatch Institute – http://www.worldwatch.org/global-plastic-production-rises-recycling-lags-0

20 Plastic Pollution in the World's Oceans: More than 5 Trillion Plastic Pieces Weighing over 250,000 Tons Afloat at Sea – http://journals.plos.org/plosone/article?id=10.1371/journal.pone.0111913

21 Ocean Gyre (Quick Facts) – Science OC – http://www.scienceoc.org/ocean-gyre-project/ocean-gyre-quick-facts

22 OR&R's Marine Debris Program – https://marinedebris.noaa.gov/info/patch.html

REFERENCES

23 10 Startling Facts About Bottled Water | Ban the Bottle – https://www.banthebottle.net/articles/10-startling-facts-about-bottled-water/

24 Magnitude of plastic waste going into the ocean calculated: 8 million metric tons of plastic enter the oceans per year – ScienceDaily – https://www.sciencedaily.com/releases/2015/02/150212154422.htm

25 Cigarette Butt Litter Fact Sheet – Tobacco Free – Lansing Community College – http://www.lcc.edu/tobaccofree/environmental

26 Marine dumping « Water Pollution Guide – http://www.water-pollution.org.uk/marine.html

27 Marine dumping « Water Pollution Guide – http://www.water-pollution.org.uk/marine.html

28 20 Facts About Ocean Pollution – Conserve Energy Future – http://www.conserve-energy-future.com/various-ocean-pollution-facts.php

29 Entanglement of Marine Species in Marine Debris with an Emphasis on Species in the United States | 2014 NOAA Marine Debris Program Report – https://marinedebris.noaa.gov/sites/default/files/mdp_entanglement.pdf

30 Drugs in the water – Harvard Health – http://www.health.harvard.edu/newsletter_article/drugs-in-the-water

31 The National Water-Quality Assessment Program – Science to Policy and Management – USGS 2010 – https://water.usgs.gov/nawqa/xrel.pdf

32 Cruise Control – A Report on how Cruise Ships Affect the Marine Environment – The Ocean Conservancy – 2002 – http://montereybay.noaa.gov/sac/2002/060702/occr53102.pdf

33 How Does Oil Get into the Ocean? | response.restoration.noaa.gov – http://response.restoration.noaa.gov/about/media/how-does-oil-get-ocean.html

34 Marine problems: Pollution | WWF – http://wwf.panda.org/about_our_earth/blue_planet/problems/pollution

35 Gulf or BP Oil Spill – http://ocean.si.edu/gulf-oil-spill

36 FAO – News Article: Key facts and findings – http://www.fao.org/news/story/en/item/197623/icode

159

37 Runoff Pollution – MISSISSIPPI DEPARTMENT OF TRANSPORTATION – http://sp.mdot.ms.gov/Maintenance/thinkgreen/Documents/Awareness/Runoff_Pollution.pdf

38 Ocean disposal of radioactive waste – Wikipedia – https://en.wikipedia.org/wiki/Ocean_disposal_of_radioactive_waste

39 All fouled up – Fukushima four years after the catastrophe – The Ecologist – http://www.theecologist.org/News/news_analysis/2782207/all_fouled_up_fukushima_four_years_after_the_catastrophe.html

40 Dumping of Nuclear and Radioactive Waste In the Oceans | Soapboxie – https://soapboxie.com/social-issues/Dumping-of-Nuclear-Waste-In-the-Oceans

41 Facts – Garbage Patch – The Great Pacific Garbage Patch and other pollution issues – http://garbagepatch.net/greatpacificoceangarbagepatchfacts

42 22 Facts About Plastic Pollution (And 10 Things We Can Do About It) – EcoWatch – http://www.ecowatch.com/22-facts-about-plastic-pollution-and-10-things-we-can-do-about-it-1881885971.html

43 99 Reasons to Stop Eating Fish – http://www.organicauthority.com/99-Reasons-Stop-Eating-Fish++

44 Unsustainable fishing | WWF – http://wwf.panda.org/about_our_earth/blue_planet/problems/problems_fishing

45 Unsustainable fishing | WWF – http://wwf.panda.org/about_our_earth/blue_planet/problems/problems_fishing

46 Illegal fishing | World Ocean Review – http://worldoceanreview.com/en/wor-2/fisheries/illegal-fishing

47 Illegal fishing | World Ocean Review – http://worldoceanreview.com/en/wor-2/fisheries/illegal-fishing

48 Dynamite Fishing – Endangered Species International – http://www.endangeredspeciesinternational.org/dynamite.html

49 Bycatch | Threats | WWF – https://www.worldwildlife.org/threats/bycatch

50 Fish as food – Marine Stewardship Council – https://www.msc.org/healthy-oceans/the-oceans-today/fish-as-food

51 Illegal Fishing | Threats | WWF –
http://www.worldwildlife.org/threats/illegal-fishing

52 Increased protection urgently needed for tunas | IUCN –
https://www.iucn.org/content/increased-protection-urgently-needed-tunas

53 Can we predict the future: juvenile finfish and their seagrass nurseries in the
Chesapeake Bay – ICES Journal of Marine Science –
https://academic.oup.com/icesjms/article/71/3/681/633484/Can-we-
predict-the-future-juvenile-finfish-and

54 Fishery Basics – Seafood Markets – NOAA –
http://sanctuaries.noaa.gov/education/voicesofthebay/pdfs/wheresold.pdf

55 Canada's Commercial Seal Slaughter 2009 – IFAW –
http://www.ifaw.org/sites/default/files/2009%20seal%20sealing.pdf

56 Canada's Commercial Seal Slaughter 2009 – IFAW –
http://www.ifaw.org/sites/default/files/2009%20seal%20sealing.pdf

57 Animal Welfare aspects of the killing and skinning of seals – Scientific
Opinion of the Panel on Animal Health and Welfare – 2007 – EFSA Journal –
Wiley Online Library –
http://onlinelibrary.wiley.com/doi/10.2903/j.efsa.2007.610/abstract

58 Sea Turtle Species | Sea Turtle Conservancy –
https://conserveturtles.org/information-sea-turtles-species-world

59 Whaling Information and Whale Hunting Facts - WDC –
http://uk.whales.org/wdc-in-action/stop-whaling

60 Bottoms up: how whale poop helps feed the ocean –
http://theconversation.com/bottoms-up-how-whale-poop-helps-feed-the-
ocean-27913

61 Vaquita | Species | WWF – https://www.worldwildlife.org/species/vaquita

62 Why Are Whales Important? – http://www.whalefacts.org/why-are-whales-
important

63 Sea Turtle Deaths Caused By Shrimping Industry Prompts Lawsuit | The
Huffington Post – http://www.huffingtonpost.com/2015/04/15/sea-turtle-
deaths-shrimping-lawsuit_n_7073466.html

64 WWF Climate Change –
http://wwf.panda.org/about_our_earth/blue_planet/problems/climate_change

65 WWF Report 2015 – Living Blue Planet Report Species, habitats and human
well-being –
http://awsassets.wwf.org.au/downloads/mo038_living_blue_planet_report
_16sep15.pdf

66 In Dead Water | GRID-Arendal – Publications –
http://www.grida.no/publications/rr/in-dead-water/page/1244.aspx

67 Facts About The Great Barrier Reef –
http://www.greatbarrierreef.org/about-the-reef/great-barrier-reef-facts

68 The Eleventh International Seagrass Biology Workshop –
http://isbw11.csp.escience.cn/dct/page/1

69 Vital marine habitat under threat : Nature News –
http://www.nature.com/news/2009/090629/full/news.2009.608.html

70 Seagrass and Seagrass Beds | Smithsonian Ocean Portal –
http://ocean.si.edu/seagrass-and-seagrass-beds

71 Mangrove Forests: One of the World's Threatened Major Tropical
Environments – Simon Fraser University –
http://www.sfu.ca/~ianh/geog315/readings/Valiela.pdf

72 Climate Change from ThankYouOcean –
http://thankyouocean.org/threats/climate-change

73 EPA Climate Change – https://www.epa.gov/climate-change-science/causes-
climate-change

74 Paris Agreement on Climate Action
https://ec.europa.eu/clima/policies/international/negotiations/paris_en

75 Over 50% of the World's Population is Under 30 – Social Media on the Rise |
Socialnomics – http://socialnomics.net/2010/04/13/over-50-of-the-worlds-
population-is-under-30-social-media-on-the-rise

76 Marine defaunation: Animal loss in the global ocean | Science –
http://science.sciencemag.org/content/347/6219/1255641

77 Marine defaunation: Animal loss in the global ocean | Science –
   http://science.sciencemag.org/content/347/6219/1255641

78 Blue Carbon | *Humanitarian News* –
   http://humanitariannews.org/20161125/blue-carbon

79 Seagrass and Seagrass Beds | Smithsonian Ocean Portal –
   http://ocean.si.edu/seagrass-and-seagrass-beds

80 Seagrass and Seagrass Beds | Smithsonian Ocean Portal –
   http://ocean.si.edu/seagrass-and-seagrass-beds

81 Global Atlas of Marine Fisheries – https://islandpress.org/book/global-atlas-
   of-marine-fisheries

82 In Dead Water | GRID-Arendal – Publications –
   http://www.grida.no/publications/rr/in-dead-water

83 Plastics – the facts 2015 by PlasticsEurope – issuu –
   https://issuu.com/plasticseuropeebook/docs/finalplasticsthefacts2015eboo
   kwebve

84 In Dead Water | GRID-Arendal – Publications –
   http://www.grida.no/publications/rr/in-dead-water

85 Plastic to outweigh fish in oceans by 2050, study warns –
   https://phys.org/news/2016-01-plastic-outweigh-fish-oceans.html

ACKNOWLEDGEMENTS

Working on this project and writing this book, my first, has been a wonderful experience. The amount of energy I've generated and released by doing this has far exceeded my expectations. This is just the beginning.

Words cannot describe the strong bond my family has. Having lived abroad for many years, we – for good and for bad – have always helped each other out. No matter what. I am extremely grateful for that. A million hugs and kisses for Hilde, Lucas and Sophie.

Kevin McLoughlin, Jim Green, Debbie Jenkins and the entire team at Orca Scuba, you guys have been amazing, channelling and controlling my craziness, delivering loads of information and never holding back. Actually, this has been a lot of fun. I am sure we will be launching more books – creating positive footprints.

Last but not least, thanks to my amazing team of 'proof readers' and supporters. In random order: William Shaw, Anna Green, Kelly Timmins, Tony Goldsmith, Inez van de Waal, Joanna Buckley, Vicky Juett, Martin Foakes, Ron Maclean, Fanny Rotsaerts, Richard 'the Inspector' Dolman, Natasha Stefanovska, Simone Wirthmann, Gaz Lyden, Elaine Brett, Duncan Journee, Owen Choo, Toby Sparrow, Matt Headen, Peter van de Waal, Joanne Wallace, Karina Schrappe-Sucre, Paula Kemp, Anne de Weert and Richard Mountain.

Photos copyright Kevin McLoughlin with additional photography from Pixabay.com

ABOUT JEROEN VAN DE WAAL

 Jeroen grew up in the East of the Netherlands – far away from the oceans. At an early age, he was intrigued and inspired by the expeditions of Jacques Cousteau and the crew of the *Calypso*. He must have watched every episode at least ten times on a little black and white television, and he dreamed of becoming a marine biologist and ocean explorer.

Around this time, he also became passionate about protecting nature and animals. This fervour was heavily fuelled by the gruesome pictures in the newspapers of the clubbing of defenceless seal pups in Canada. He couldn't understand how human beings could be so cruel simply to make hideous winter coats for rich people.

Growing up in a Robin Hood-type landscape, where scuba and diving were the exclusive, expensive and dangerous domains of exotic adventurers, Jeroen ended up studying mechanical engineering and business administration. Once he'd graduated, he got a job in fluid power. This took him all around the world to the USA, Argentina, Brazil, China and Singapore, his last ten years of corporate work being as a CEO in Asia. Living and working in all these places gave him plenty of opportunities to dive while he climbed the corporate ladder.

Working with different people, enjoying multiple cultures, languages and environments, he gained a lot of experience, business and strategic wisdom. But, something significant was missing. The strong desire and drive to follow his passion – live, thrive and dive while doing something significant and good – was haunting him. He wanted to turn the tides and give a positive outlook and hope to the younger generations, so he needed to break his complacency and rid himself of his sense of doom.

So, for the past five years, he has worked on his diving and gained certifications to become a PADI IDC Staff Instructor.

Now Jeroen is ready to put his experience to work by giving young people the tools to help reverse the destructive processes and trends that are ruining oceans, forests and wildlife as a whole. He's a firm believer that we need to disconnect from the multimedia mainstream 24/7 newsblasting info channels and reconnect with our core values. He wants to wake up tens of thousands of explorers and discoverers by instilling hope in our children and helping them learn, love and live in nature. This next generation will accelerate and innovate new ways to help nature and the oceans.

Jeroen is building an organisation that will focus on doing good. He wants to work with children, young academics, explorers, inventors, schools, universities, multinational companies and research labs. Using Orca Scuba as an accelerator, incubator and connector where people meet and get introduced to the oceanic environment, he wants to develop and build up a movement that creates educational material, protects the oceans and wildlife, enables children to become scuba divers and explorers with the ultimate goal to stop destructive and wasteful behaviour.

Together he believes we can turn the tide and put the oceans, planet and nature first.

OrcaScuba

Who we are:
Dedicated to the welfare of our oceans, the planet and all of it inhabitants. We are a multi-national collective of experienced safety conscious and environmentally aware scuba professiona with a passion for ocean conservation.

What we offer:
Entry to professional level scuba courses
Scuba programs for kids from 5 years
Special combination packages
Marine conservation programs
Certified diver packages
First aid training
Orca Yoga

Our mission:
"Turning Tides & Creating Positive Footprints" through educatio
Partnering with like-minded individuals, collectives & companie
Together creating change, one step at a time.

Where we are:
Head Quarters: Singapore
Support Office: Kuala Lumpur
Dive Center: Pulau Rawa, Malaysia
Dive Center: Pulau Weh, Indonesia

Where we are going:
Tomorrow - South East Asia
Next week – Beyond!

PADI
5 STAR
INSTRUCTOR
DEVELOPMENT
CENTRE

dive@orcascuba.com   www.orcascuba.com

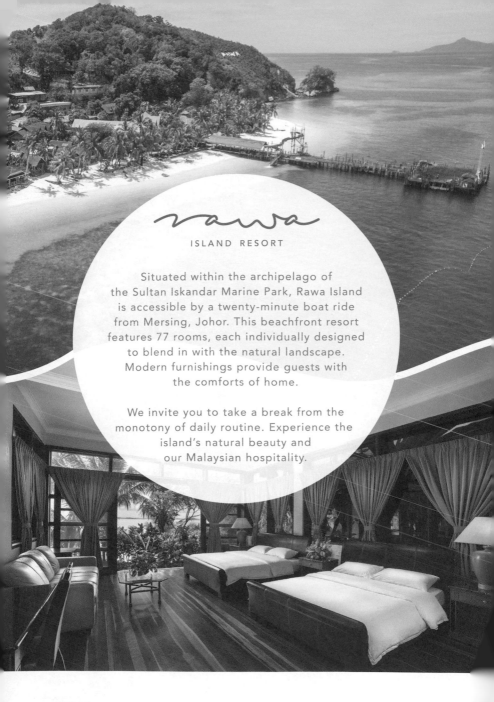

rawa
ISLAND RESORT

Situated within the archipelago of
the Sultan Iskandar Marine Park, Rawa Island
is accessible by a twenty-minute boat ride
from Mersing, Johor. This beachfront resort
features 77 rooms, each individually designed
to blend in with the natural landscape.
Modern furnishings provide guests with
the comforts of home.

We invite you to take a break from the
monotony of daily routine. Experience the
island's natural beauty and
our Malaysian hospitality.

RAWA ISLAND RESORT SDN. BHD.
Tourist Centre, Jalan Abu Bakar, 86800 Mersing, Johor, Malaysia.
Reservation Line: (607)-799 1204 / 1205   Fax: (607)-799 3848
Email: rawaisland@live.com   Website: www.rawaislandresort.co
Office Hours: 8:00 am - 5:00 pm daily

scuba store.sg

Scuba equipment, accessories & materials

Repairs & servicing

Retail, online & onsite stores

Professional advice on sizing & fitting

#02-06 Queensway Shopping Center
, Queensway, Singapore
n: +65 8339 5001
es - Sun 12:00 - 20:00
tact us to make an
intment for consultation
orcascuba.com   www.scubastore.sg

OrcaScuba

About Orca Scuba Weh

rca Scuba have teamed up with Pulau Weh Paradise to open our new dive
enter at their resort on the beautiful island, Pulau Weh or "moving island"
just off the northern most tip of Sumatra, in Aceh province, Indonesia.

Why Weh?

is volcanic island has a lot to offer for those seeking adventure. The rocky
rain is covered in lush jungle & due to its protected status it is home to an
abundance of wildlife such as monkeys, wild boar & monitor lizards
to name but a few.

Why Diving?

istine reefs teem with a huge variety of marine life! Reef fish, nudibranch,
turtles, moray eels & even some big pelagic life can be seen.
The ocean here really hassomething for everyone, shallow easy dives
close to shore for those that are still at beginner level & some exciting
drift & deep dives for those with more experience.

Book your next dive adventure now at dive@orcascuba.com

OrcaScuba

Started in Singapore where our corporate HQ and first
Customer Connection Center (CCC) is based.

Next we opened our flagship PADI 5 star IDC and conservation center on Pulau Rawa, Malay

Now, our continued success has allowed us to expand and open a new CCC in Kuala Lumpt
Malaysia and dive centers on Pulau Weh, Indonesia and on Koh Tao in the gulf of Thailanc

Through a stringent selection process, we have nominated Orca Scuba accredited partner c
centers and live aboard dive boat operators in prime locations throughout South East Asia

As our success continues and with your help we will continue to spread our love for the oce
and its inhabitants as far as we can through scuba dive training & marine conservation.

Keep up to date with our expansion by checking our website www.orcascuba.com
and following our blog, newsletter or social media channels.

Look out for our coloured O symbols denoting the different type of Orca facilities.
Today South East Asia, tomorrow beyond!